D1294790

STATE PROFILES

INDIANA

BY BETSY RATHBURN

BELLWETHER MEDIA • MINNEAPOLIS, MN

Blastoff! Discovery launches a new mission: reading to learn. Filled with facts and features, each book offers you an exciting new world to explore!

BLASTOFF! UNIVERSE

BLASTOFF! Beginners — GRADE K

BLASTOFF! READERS — GRADES 1-3

BLASTOFF! DISCOVERY — GRADE 4

This edition first published in 2022 by Bellwether Media, Inc.

No part of this publication may be reproduced in whole or in part without written permission of the publisher.
For information regarding permission, write to Bellwether Media, Inc., Attention: Permissions Department,
6012 Blue Circle Drive, Minnetonka, MN 55343.

Library of Congress Cataloging-in-Publication Data

Names: Rathburn, Betsy, author.
Title: Indiana / by Betsy Rathburn.
Description: Minneapolis, MN : Bellwether Media, Inc., 2022. | Series: Blastoff! Discovery: State profiles | Includes bibliographical references and index. | Audience: Ages 7-13 | Audience: Grades 4-6 | Summary: "Engaging images accompany information about Indiana. The combination of high-interest subject matter and narrative text is intended for students in grades 3 through 8"– Provided by publisher.
Identifiers: LCCN 2021019671 (print) | LCCN 2021019672 (ebook) | ISBN 9781644873854 (library binding) | ISBN 9781648341625 (ebook)
Subjects: LCSH: Indiana–Juvenile literature.
Classification: LCC F526.3 .R38 2022 (print) | LCC F526.3 (ebook) | DDC 977.2–dc23
LC record available at https://lccn.loc.gov/2021019671
LC ebook record available at https://lccn.loc.gov/2021019672

Editor: Colleen Sexton   Designer: Laura Sowers

Printed in the United States of America, North Mankato, MN.

TABLE OF CONTENTS

THE INDIANAPOLIS ZOO

ABOUT THE ANIMALS

The Indianapolis Zoo is home to more than 1,400 animals. Visitors can experience about 200 species found around the world!

A family steps inside the gates of the Indianapolis Zoo. They start with the shark touch pool. It is the biggest pool of its kind in the United States. The family runs their hands along the smooth backs of dogfish sharks. In a nearby aquarium, they watch angelfish and tangs swim among the colorful **corals**.

ANGEL MOUNDS STATE HISTORIC SITE

INDIANA DUNES NATIONAL PARK

INDIANAPOLIS MOTOR SPEEDWAY

TURKEY RUN STATE PARK

Next, the family helps feed the giraffes. The giraffes use their long tongues to lick food from visitors' hands. After the feeding, the family visits zebras, African elephants, and cheetahs. The Indianapolis Zoo is full of amazing animals. Welcome to Indiana!

Indiana is the smallest state in the **Midwest** region of the United States. This tall, narrow state covers 36,420 square miles (94,327 square kilometers). Indiana's capital, Indianapolis, lies in the center of the state along the White River. Many major roads meet in the capital. Other large Indiana cities include Fort Wayne, Evansville, and South Bend.

Ohio borders Indiana to the east. To the south, the Ohio River separates Indiana from Kentucky. Illinois lies west of Indiana. Michigan is the state's northern neighbor. Lake Michigan washes about 45 miles (72 kilometers) of Indiana's northern border.

ILLINOIS

LAKE MICHIGAN

MICHIGAN

SOUTH BEND

FORT WAYNE

OHIO

INDIANA

INDIANAPOLIS

WHITE RIVER

OHIO RIVER

KENTUCKY

EVANSVILLE

7

People have lived in Indiana for thousands of years. Over time, they formed Native American tribes, including the Potawatomi, Delaware, Miami, and Shawnee. Many of these groups joined together to form the **Miami Confederation** in the 1600s. The Confederation fought to protect lands from the invading Iroquois people.

ANGEL MOUNDS

About 1,000 years ago, Mississippian peoples built southern Indiana's famous Angel Mounds. The largest of the mounds is 44 feet (13 meters) tall!

French explorers arrived in northern Indiana in 1679. Fur traders soon built **settlements** along rivers. Indiana became a U.S. **territory** after the **Revolutionary War**. The U.S. government began forcing Native Americans in Indiana to give up their land and move into western territories. More settlers arrived after Indiana became the 19th state in 1816.

NATIVE PEOPLES OF INDIANA

MIAMI NATION OF INDIANA

- Original lands in Indiana, Illinois, and southern Michigan, and later, Ohio
- Many Miami were forced out of Indiana in 1846, and their relatives live in Oklahoma today
- About 6,000 Miami Indians in Indiana today

POKAGON BAND OF POTAWATOMI

- Original lands in the Great Lakes region
- Most Potawatomi were forced westward in the 1830s, but the Pokagon and other small bands remained
- Today, the Pokagon Band's 5,000 members live in northern Indiana and southwestern Michigan

The Great Lakes **Plain** covers northern Indiana. Sand **dunes** rise along Lake Michigan. Farther south, the land flattens into farmland dotted with lakes. The state's richest farmland lies in the Till Plains of central Indiana. The Wabash River flows across this region and turns southward near the Illinois border to meet the Ohio River. The south is hilly. In some places, lowlands stretch between steep hills called knobs.

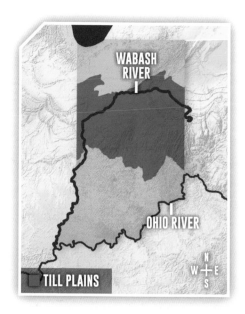

WABASH RIVER

OHIO RIVER

TILL PLAINS

N
W + E
S

INDIANA'S CHALLENGE: CLIMATE CHANGE

Hoosiers are experiencing the effects of climate change. Rising temperatures dry out lakes and rivers, while heavy rain and snow cause flooding. These conditions make corn harvests smaller, which leads to lower earnings for farmers and less food for animals.

WABASH RIVER

SPRING
HIGH: 62°F (17°C)
LOW: 41°F (5°C)

SUMMER
HIGH: 84°F (29°C)
LOW: 63°F (17°C)

FALL
HIGH: 64°F (18°C)
LOW: 44°F (7°C)

WINTER
HIGH: 37°F (3°C)
LOW: 21°F (-6°C)

°F = degrees Fahrenheit
°C = degrees Celsius

Indiana has four seasons. Summers are warm and muggy. Spring often brings thunderstorms and tornadoes. Fall is mild, and winter is cold and snowy. Areas along Lake Michigan often get heavier snow than the rest of the state.

11

Indiana is full of wildlife! The state bird is the northern cardinal. In winter and spring, bright red males are easy to spot on bare branches. Indiana bats swoop from caves in search of beetles and butterflies. In fields and forests, quails and wild turkeys peck at the ground. White-tailed deer dash away from bobcats.

Cottontail rabbits, raccoons, and skunks make homes in forests. There, timber rattlesnakes lie in wait for their next meal. Sunfish, bass, and trout fill Indiana's rivers and lakes. Painted turtles sunbathe on rocks. Beavers and muskrats chew plants in shallow waters.

WHITE-TAILED DEER

COTTONTAIL RABBIT

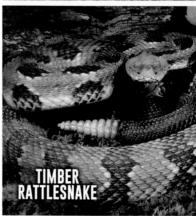

TIMBER RATTLESNAKE

MIDLAND PAINTED TURTLE

MUSKRAT

12

NORTHERN CARDINAL

Life Span: up to 15 years
Status: least concern

northern cardinal range =

LEAST CONCERN	NEAR THREATENED	VULNERABLE	ENDANGERED	CRITICALLY ENDANGERED	EXTINCT IN THE WILD	EXTINCT

13

PEOPLE AND COMMUNITIES

Around 6.8 million people live in Indiana. They are called Hoosiers. About 3 of every 4 Hoosiers live in cities. The rest live in **rural** areas. Most Hoosiers have **ancestors** from Germany, Ireland, England, and other European countries. About 1 in 10 are African American or Black. Gary, East Chicago, and Indianapolis are home to strong African American communities.

INDIANA'S CHALLENGE: DRINKING WATER

More than half of Indiana's rivers and lakes are polluted. Water is cleaned before it reaches homes. But more pollution may make water harder to clean. The state may need new ways to make its water safe to drink.

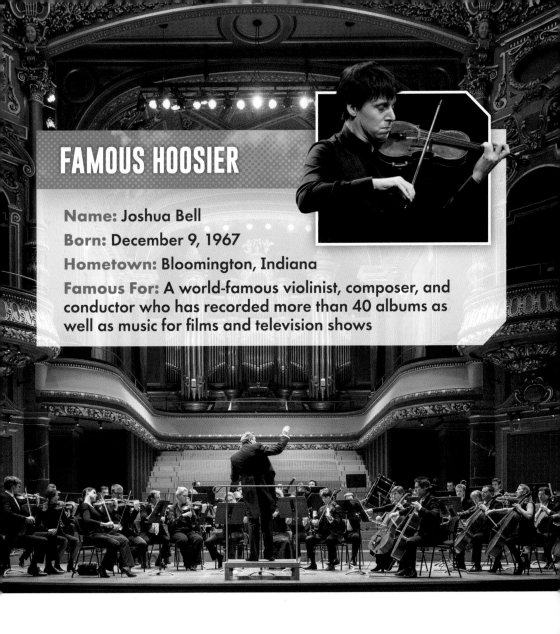

FAMOUS HOOSIER

Name: Joshua Bell

Born: December 9, 1967

Hometown: Bloomington, Indiana

Famous For: A world-famous violinist, composer, and conductor who has recorded more than 40 albums as well as music for films and television shows

Smaller numbers of Hoosiers are Hispanic, Asian American, and Native American. The Pokagon Band of Potawatomi Indians and the Miami people both have land in Indiana. Recent **immigrants** have come from Mexico, India, and China.

Indianapolis is Indiana's largest city and capital. It sits in the center of the state where the White River meets Fall Creek. Delaware Indians and small groups of European settlers lived in the area before it became the capital in 1825.

Indianapolis's downtown area, known as Mile Square, features Monument Circle surrounded by office towers. Bicyclists follow the Indianapolis **Cultural** Trail through the city. It winds past museums, restaurants, and theaters. The Old National Centre hosts many concerts and plays. Newfields is home to a nature park and the Indianapolis Museum of Art. The museum holds more than 54,000 works of art!

THE WORLD'S LARGEST

The Children's Museum of Indianapolis is the largest children's museum in the world. Its most popular exhibit is Dinosphere, where dinosaur skeletons tower over visitors!

MONUMENT CIRCLE

Rich soil has always been important to Indiana's economy. Early settlers grew crops and raised livestock. Farmers began trading their goods with other states when railroads arrived in Indiana. Today, corn and soybeans are Indiana's most valuable farm products. Farmers also raise hogs, cattle, and turkeys.

AT A CROSSROADS

Many interstate highways run through Indiana. Trucks travel these roads to transport products across the United States. For this reason, Indiana is often called the Crossroads of America!

Manufacturing is big business in Indiana. Factory workers produce steel for automakers. They also make electronic parts, furniture, and medicines. In the southwest, miners dig up coal. Most Hoosiers have **service jobs**. They work in hospitals, schools, and banks. The state government also employs many service workers.

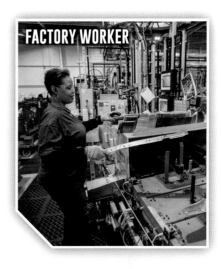

FACTORY WORKER

INVENTED IN INDIANA

ELECTRIC GARAGE DOOR OPENER
Date Invented: 1926
Inventor: C.G. Johnson

PUSH LAWN MOWER
Date Invented: 1870
Inventor: Elwood McGuire

SUDOKU PUZZLE
Date Invented: 1979
Inventor: Howard Garns

GASOLINE PUMP
Date Invented: 1885
Inventor: Sylvanus Bowser

PORK TENDERLOIN SANDWICH

Hoosiers enjoy hearty dishes. The popular pork tenderloin sandwich reflects the state's German **heritage**. A thin slice of meat is breaded, fried, and served on a bun. Many Hoosiers enjoy chicken and noodles served over mashed potatoes. Cooks fry or bake walleye and other lake fish. A popular breakfast features sausage gravy poured over buttery biscuits.

SAUSAGE GRAVY AND BISCUITS

Favorite Indiana desserts include Hoosier pie. This creamy, sugary dessert created by the **Amish** community is a popular state fair food. Persimmon pudding is another sweet treat. It mixes cream, sugar, and persimmon fruit into a moist cake.

PERSIMMON PUDDING

HOOSIER PIE

6-8
SERVINGS

Ask an adult to help you make Indiana's official state dessert!

INGREDIENTS

9-inch piecrust, baked

4 tablespoons cornstarch

3/4 cup white sugar

2 1/4 cups half and half

6 tablespoons butter, melted

1 teaspoon vanilla extract

1/2 teaspoon ground cinnamon

DIRECTIONS

1. Mix the cornstarch and sugar. Add the half and half and 4 tablespoons of melted butter.

2. Cook over medium heat. Stir constantly until the mixture boils and becomes thick and creamy.

3. Remove from heat and stir in the vanilla extract.

4. Preheat the oven broiler to high.

5. Pour the mixture into the piecrust. Drizzle 2 tablespoons of melted butter over the top and sprinkle with cinnamon.

6. Put the pie under the broiler for a few minutes, until the butter bubbles.

7. Refrigerate for at least 1 hour before serving.

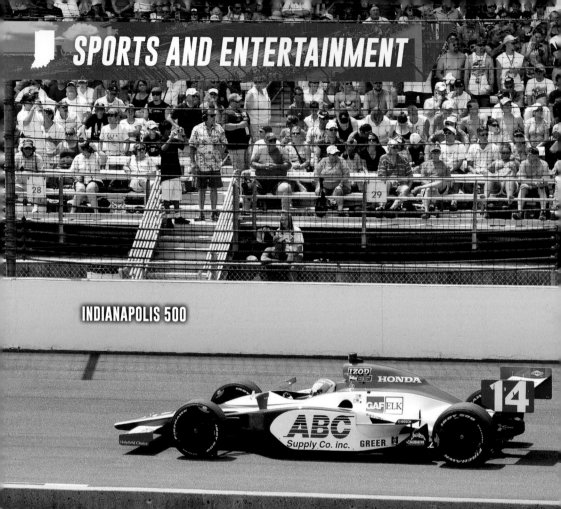

SPORTS AND ENTERTAINMENT

INDIANAPOLIS 500

Indiana is full of fun things to do! In summer, Hoosiers enjoy camping, hiking, and fishing in Indiana's state parks. Winter brings out cross-country skiers and ice skaters. Concerts and community theater performances draw audiences throughout the state.

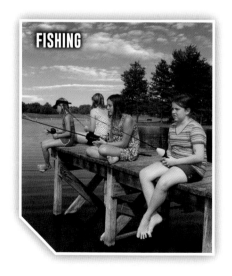

FISHING

Hoosiers are big sports fans. College basketball is especially popular. Indiana University's Hoosiers have won many championships. Crowds also cheer for the state's professional basketball teams, the Indiana Pacers and the Indiana Fever. In fall and winter, Hoosiers root for the Indianapolis Colts football team. The Indianapolis 500 each spring is a major event. Around 300,000 people fill the stands for this exciting auto race.

NOTABLE SPORTS TEAM

Indiana Pacers
Sport: National Basketball Association
Started: 1967
Place of Play: Bankers Life Fieldhouse

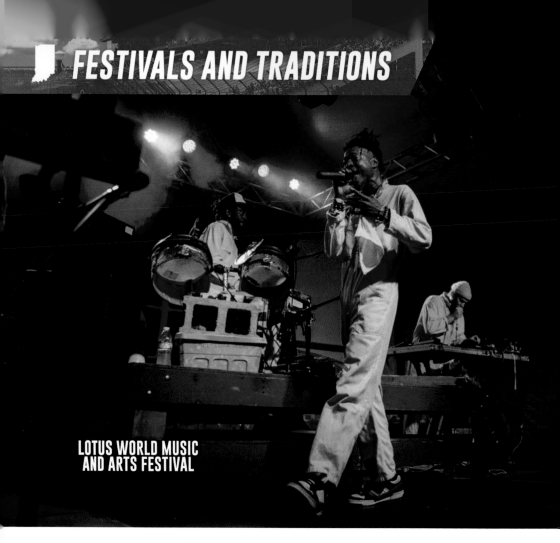

LOTUS WORLD MUSIC
AND ARTS FESTIVAL

Hoosiers come together for many festivals each year. The town of Peru hosts the annual Circus City Festival every summer. **Trapeze artists** thrill audiences with high-flying stunts. Hoosiers end the summer with the Indiana State Fair. Rides, games, concerts, and barnyard animals bring out huge crowds.

INDIANA STATE FAIR

In September, the Lotus World Music and Arts Festival in Bloomington features performers from around the world. At the Marshall County Blueberry Festival in September, residents enjoy fireworks, car shows, and blueberry pies. In October, the Indiana **Ethnic** Expo in Columbus features food and entertainment from countries around the world. There is plenty to celebrate in the Hoosier State!

TAKE THE PLUNGE!

At the Wawasee Winter Carnival, brave Hoosiers take the polar plunge. They jump into an icy lake to raise money for the community!

INDIANA ETHNIC EXPO

1783
The United States wins the Revolutionary War, gaining the land that is now Indiana

1825
Indianapolis becomes Indiana's state capital

1600s
Native American groups form the Miami Confederation

1679
René-Robert Cavelier, Sieur de La Salle, of France is the first European to explore Indiana

1816
Indiana becomes the 19th state

2007

The Indianapolis Colts win
Super Bowl XLI

1911

The first Indianapolis 500
race is held

1846

The U.S. government
forcefully removes the
Miami people from Indiana

2017

Former Indiana governor
Mike Pence becomes vice
president of the United States

1977

Julia Carson and Katie Hall
become the first African
American women to serve
in the Indiana Senate

INDIANA FACTS

Nickname: The Hoosier State

Motto: The Crossroads of America

Date of Statehood: December 11, 1816
(the 19th state)

Capital City: Indianapolis ★

Other Major Cities: Fort Wayne, Evansville, South Bend

Area: 36,420 square miles (94,327 square kilometers);
Indiana is the 38th largest state.

Population

6,785,528
(2020)

STATE FLAG

Indiana's flag is dark blue with a gold torch in the middle. The torch stands for freedom and enlightenment. An outer ring of 13 stars and an inner ring of 5 stars surround the torch. The outer ring represents the 13 original colonies. The inner stars stand for the next 5 states to join the United States. At the top of the torch is a larger gold star with *Indiana* written above it. This star stands for Indiana, the 19th state.

INDUSTRY

Main Exports

machinery

corn

medicine

car parts

electronic parts

pigs

JOBS

MANUFACTURING
14%

FARMING AND NATURAL RESOURCES
2%

GOVERNMENT
12%

SERVICES
72%

Natural Resources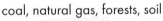
coal, natural gas, forests, soil

GOVERNMENT

Federal Government

9 REPRESENTATIVES | **2** SENATORS

IN

11 ELECTORAL VOTES

USA

State Government

100 REPRESENTATIVES | **50** SENATORS

STATE SYMBOLS

STATE BIRD
NORTHERN CARDINAL

STATE INSECT
SAY'S FIREFLY

STATE FLOWER
PEONY

STATE TREE
TULIP POPLAR

Amish—a Christian group that came to North America from Switzerland and Germany in the 1700s

ancestors—relatives who lived long ago

corals—the living ocean animals that build coral reefs

cultural—relating to the beliefs, arts, and ways of life in a place or society

dunes—hills of sand

ethnic—related to a group of people who share customs and an identity

heritage—the traditions, achievements, and beliefs that are part of the history of a group of people

immigrants—people who move to a new country

manufacturing—a field of work in which people use machines to make products

Miami Confederation—a group of eight Native American nations; the Miami and the Potawatomi were the most powerful tribes of the confederation.

Midwest—a region of 12 states in the north-central United States

plain—a large area of flat land

Revolutionary War—the war from 1775 to 1783 in which the United States fought for independence from Great Britain

rural—related to the countryside

service jobs—jobs that perform tasks for people or businesses

settlements—places where newly arrived people live

territory—an area of land under the control of a government; territories in the United States are considered part of the country but do not have power in the government.

trapeze artists—people who perform on horizontal bars suspended in the air

AT THE LIBRARY

Bodden, Valerie. *Shawnee*. Mankato, Minn.: Creative Education, 2020.

Orr, Tamra B. *Indiana*. New York, N.Y.: Children's Press, 2018.

Whiting, Jim. *The Story of the Indianapolis Colts*. Mankato, Minn.: Creative Education, 2020.

ON THE WEB

FACTSURFER

Factsurfer.com gives you a safe, fun way to find more information.

1. Go to www.factsurfer.com.

2. Enter "Indiana" into the search box and click ⌕.

3. Select your book cover to see a list of related content.

INDEX